*Favorite people
carry each other
in their hearts...
forever and always.*

I Thanked God for You Today

*Words of Appreciation
and Support for Someone
Who Means So Much*

Donna Fargo

Blue Mountain Press™
Boulder, Colorado

Dedication

This book is dedicated to all the special people who enrich our lives and whose happiness and well-being we care so much about. It's a way to let them know that they are in our thoughts and prayers.

— Donna Fargo

Library of Congress Control Number: 2009910108
ISBN: 978-1-59842-474-4

◪ and Blue Mountain Press are registered in U.S. Patent and Trademark Office.
Certain trademarks are used under license.

Printed in China.
Second Printing: 2011

♻ This book is printed on recycled paper.

This book is printed on paper that has been specially produced to be acid free (neutral pH) and contains no groundwood or unbleached pulp. It conforms with the requirements of the American National Standards Institute, Inc., so as to ensure that this book will last and be enjoyed by future generations.

Blue Mountain Arts, Inc.
P.O. Box 4549, Boulder, Colorado 80306

Contents

I Thanked God
for You
Today

You're one of my heart's favorite people, and I want you to know that today I thanked God for your presence in my life. I said a prayer of gratitude for your understanding and thoughtfulness, your generosity and sensitivity. I expressed my thanks for the smiles you bring to my world and the sunshine you add to my days. I am so fortunate we have each other to share the everyday stuff of life. You make me feel connected, appreciated, and accepted, and I'm so thankful for you.

Today I wished you an abundance of love and joy, good health, and the best of everything. I prayed that you would have the kind of faith and wisdom you need to accomplish anything and everything you desire. I wished you happiness.

People who enrich our lives are such a blessing. I consider you a treasure that I would never want to lose.

I thanked God for you today.

I Would Need
a New Language
to Tell You How Much
You Mean to Me

You and I have walked through life together. We know that the other one is there… to share the highs and the lows and everything else.

We are connected at the heart, and our commitment to each other is permanent. We believe in each other. We are sensitive and supportive, and we can talk about anything. We each know the other will understand, no matter what.

We aren't afraid to break the rules, defend each other, and go out of our way.

We've cried together and laughed together, and we have been there when it mattered.

Our loyalty is strong and lasting, and our bond is unquestionable and unconditional. We know that we'll keep on being there through everything life has in store for us.

I need some new words to tell you how thankful I am for you, but I hope these old ones will let you know that no one can take your place in my life—ever. You will always live in my heart.

*I Have So Many
Wishes for You
I Can't Even
Count Them, but
Here Are Just a Few...*

I wish you light to get you through every dark place and arms to hold you when you need to feel loved. I wish you enough faith to believe in miracles. I wish you everything you need to make you happy.

I wish you satisfaction in your work, recognition for all the good you do, and fearless enthusiasm for everything you try to do. May there be harmony, unconditional acceptance, and understanding in your family.

Everyone is unique and different. You're an angel in disguise to some, a friend so important to others, and a member of a family to whom you have significance beyond description.

Special people help us change our lives; they make us feel good about ourselves and give us a sense of community and belonging. You are that kind of person to me, and today I asked God to bless you and keep you always.

You Mean the World to Me

There are people in our lives who help us keep our balance so we don't alienate ourselves from the world. They make us feel supported so we don't give up when we're having a hard time. They help us translate confusion into a language we understand. We share our heart space with them, and they help us with our emotional well-being. They make our lives more pleasant.

All of this brings me to you… You have taught me so much. You show your concern for whatever matters to me, and you appreciate the things I do for you. We value each other's counsel and ideas and help each other make wiser decisions. We have fun together. We can be blatantly honest with each other because we've been tested and retested. We know each other so well that we don't have to say a word sometimes.

I don't know what I would do without you to complain to and act crazy with. You're sensitive to my moods, and you stand by me when I need you to. You lend me your shoulder to cry on. You laugh with me when life's not all that funny and I get caught in some mess. You keep your promises. You build bridges instead of walls. You treat me right all the time. You're my safe haven in this unfriendly world, my buddy to walk with through the storms. You mean the world to me.

I Know
We'll Always
Be There
for Each Other

I know we will be there for each other during all the seasons of our lives, no matter where the road takes us. I can't imagine a circumstance that I would not be around for you or a place in time that I would not want you there with me.

When the world is not making much sense for you, I will row with you against the tide. When you're adjusting and adapting, I'll be there for you until you reach your goal. I will pray for you when you need me to, just like I know you've done for me so many times. We'll be each other's anchor to keep us grounded and secure.

Having you in my life is one of the best things that has ever happened to me. I have grown to trust you and care about you, and I love sharing the time we spend together. Knowing you lifts me up. You fill an empty space in my heart, and I hope you will stay in my life forever.

We Share a Unique Connection

When two people really feel "connected," it's almost like a spiritual alliance between two souls. It's hard to explain why, but life just has more rhythm and melody. That's the kind of connection I feel with you.

We've invested our time and energy in each other and developed a bond that has evolved naturally over the years. We stay in touch; we call; we talk to each other about what's going on. We're on the same wavelength, and it feels good to have someone who knows where we've been, where we are now, and where we want to go.

We thrive on an exchange of loyalty and encouragement, goodwill, and unconditional trust. We do favors for each other—not because we're obligated but because we want to—and we stay committed to each other because we care about our relationship.

I'm convinced I can never really convey how much you mean to me, but there's something inside my heart that wants to let you know.

Having someone in life like you is like being given a special blessing. Even when I don't ask, you know when to be there, and you never mind going out of your way for me. I know I can always depend on you, and you can depend on me.

I am thankful to have you in my life, and I hope we will always stay close.

I'd Do Anything
for You...
If I Could

If I could help you reach your goals, supply
    your every need… I would.
If I could put magic in every day for you and
    give you everything you want… I would.
    I really would.

If I could heal every hurt you've ever known
    and help you solve every problem you have…
    I would.
If I could promise you a perfect future, help
    you live your life with no regrets… I would.
    I really would.

I can't do all that, but…
I can wish and hope and pray with you that you
    will find a way.
I can be there with you through life's ups and
    downs.
And I can encourage you and support you
    and remind you just how deserving you
    really are.
That's what I can do… and will keep on doing!

A Few Life Lessons to Guide You on the Road to Your Dreams

Treasure your dreams; like your life, they are yours and only yours, and there is a reason they're in your heart. Realize that you're the one most responsible for making them come true. Embrace this role as you move on—perhaps into uncharted territory. Be on your side as you create the map to reach your goals.

Choose your thoughts, because if you don't, you're still making a choice and you'll have to take what you get. In your mind's eye, create a positive picture that will draw what you want to you. Your intuition is powerful; use it. Maintain a burning commitment to succeed. Don't be afraid to take careful chances.

Inform yourself. Make the connection between your thoughts, your actions, and the results you're getting. The cumulative quality of your actions will weave the tapestry of your destiny. Live your life consciously.

Keep a close watch over your perspective. Acknowledge your good fortune, and don't overestimate every conflict. Look at your circumstances as life lessons. You are a student in the school of life and in many ways your own teacher. Appreciate what you've learned, and enjoy life, others, and yourself.

I Send You
Good Thoughts
Every Day

I know you can't read my mind, but I wish you could receive all the good thoughts I send your way. If you could hear all the prayers I pray for you and the many times I ask God to protect you, you'd know how much I care.

I hope you're being good to yourself, staying healthy, and loving life. I hope you're turning all the negatives into positives and finding new ways to make every day adventurous and exciting.

When I think of you, I always hope your life is just the way you want it, that you are looking forward to each day with a grateful, open heart, and that you are happy. I hope you have enough confidence to do whatever you're trying to do. Remember that anything is possible and you are more than able to handle whatever comes along.

I've Learned So Much from You

Other people may come and go, but I'm thankful you and I are in each other's life to stay.

I've learned so much from you by your example... like how to be there for someone every day. When there are problems to solve, you reach out to help. Your good judgment translates into knowing how much or how little to offer, what to say and do, and when to back off to allow for someone's privacy. Loyalty is second nature to you, and I see it in the way you share my hopes and fears, my failures and successes.

You have taught me so much about life. When you're disappointed in others, you don't give up on them. You always find a way to come through every battle a little stronger. You respect others' choices. It's clear that you have a deep regard for all of life.

You have shown me about the importance of encouragement… about helping others jump-start their motivation. You've inspired me by your words many times, probably without your even knowing it. You've taught me about being truthful and trustworthy and considerate. So many people aren't, but you are, and I appreciate that. You always practice the Golden Rule, a code of conduct that I believe in so much.

I respect you, I care for you, and I've learned so much from you. Thank you for touching my life with your amazing soul.

You Have Such
a Beautiful Spirit

You are such a rare person. I don't know where to begin to name all your good qualities because you have so many...

You're understanding and compassionate and easy to be around. You're inclusive and unselfish. You give others the benefit of the doubt, and you never seem to harbor bad feelings.

You lift others up and make them feel better when they're in your company. You know how to sift through what's on the surface and bring out the good in others. Your wisdom and sensitivity make you one of my very favorite people. You're fun to hang out with and a joy to know.

Nobody needs a magnifying glass to see your good qualities. They shine like new money and solid gold. If there were more people like you, the world would be a better place: friendlier, easier, and happier.

You have such a beautiful spirit, and I'm glad we get to live on this planet together.

You Can Do Anything!

Believe that…
Doors that are closed will also open. Where there's a will, there's a way. You have the answers inside you to every question you have. Determination gets results, persistence counts, and your attitude matters. You can make a difference—positive or negative—in your life and in your world.

Be assured that…
There's power in faith, and all things are possible. Thinking and hoping are more important when they give birth to action. You are rewarded for your efforts and your faith. God is on your side, not against you. Your life is a gift to you, but you must take responsibility for its quality.

Trust that…
Any problems you face are challenges in life,
not punishments from God. You can choose
peace no matter what you're experiencing.
Motivation and sacrifice often work together to
help move you forward. Desire and awareness
create the way for positive change. When
your words and actions are in sync, there's no
stopping you.

You have the power to do whatever you want.
Believe it!

I Wish You Could See Yourself the Way I See You

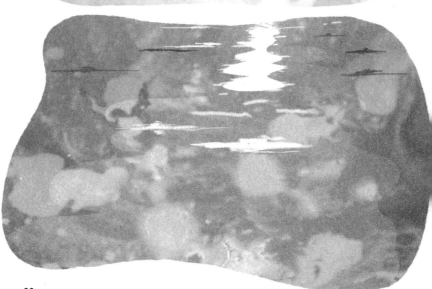

When I look at you, I see this incredible person with a tender spirit and a sharp mind. I see someone who loves life and others. I see a heart full of optimism—a person who believes in possibilities and is not distracted by fears and doubts.

I see an exemplary role model to others, someone who is strong and hopeful, tough and resilient, and whose mere presence is uplifting. You've never been stingy with your praise, and a vote of confidence from you is like super sunshine to my soul.

In you, I see someone who doesn't just talk the talk but also walks the walk. You never give up on the important things you're trying to get done, and if sometimes you miss the mark, you're the first one to get up, dust yourself off, and start over.

If you could see yourself through my eyes, you would see a person so deserving of admiration and love and appreciation.

There Will Be Times in Life That Test Your Purpose

Even when things don't seem to be working out for the best, stay committed to what you want to accomplish. Take advantage of every surprise detour you have to take to help you discover who you are. What may seem like a disappointment at the time may just be fate intervening on your behalf to keep you moving toward your destiny. Remember that "down" is just a place and you won't be there forever, but don't forget to learn all you can while you're there.

Focus on your goals, but keep an open mind. Be receptive enough to recognize an opportunity you might not have imagined, and be flexible enough to go in a different direction if you need to. Don't be discouraged.

Don't let one mistake or one result define you. Don't let one disappointment make you think you've lost the war when it was only a single battle. If you find yourself making a mountain out of a molehill, adjust. Be objective and give proper weight or value to your circumstances. Making wiser decisions in the face of conflict helps you get to know yourself better and gives you a better result. Consciously changing your attitude from frustration to fascination will empower you. Don't worry. If you can imagine it, you can have it. Find new ways to look at the mountain from the other side.

Be patient, keep on doing your best, and expect the best to come to you.

You Are
Stronger
Than You
May Think

You're like one of those strong and sturdy trees in the forest. You have experienced the winds of change and challenge, and you are still standing. Like that big tree's roots reach down into the earth, your foundation of faith and spirituality will keep you firmly planted.

When you've done all you think you can, stay determined. When you're doubtful and frustrated, don't give up. When you can't see tomorrow, just get through today.

Keep on keeping on. You will win. Don't despair. Storms and inclement weather made that big tree strong. It stood against force and resistance, and it's still standing—just like you.

You may sometimes have questions. Reach beyond your human limitations to explore the absolute miracle of the universe. Know that you're a part of it and that you have unlimited potential. Trust that you will find your answers. Know without a doubt that all things are possible, and you will be empowered to survive every trial triumphantly.

Hold On to Your Dreams, and Remember the ABCs of a Healthy Body, Mind, and Soul

Accept the things you can't change.

Be nice and be as good as your word.

Count your blessings often.

Dream like your life depends on it.

Embrace differences.

Favorite people deserve favorite treatment.

God is with you all the time; talk to Him often.

Happiness and a positive attitude are essential for a healthy mind.

Inspiration is the heart of creativity; it is the language of your spirit loving you.

Judge yourself but don't judge others.

Know what your purpose is and live it.

Love always; it's what makes life so beautiful.

Money's okay, but joy and contentment are better.

No is not always a negative word, especially when
    it could save your life.
Only you can make habits and only you can
    break them.
Practice the Golden Rule… it's always the right
    thing to do.
Quell your anger with prayer.
Respect your body by eating healthy foods and
    thinking happy thoughts.
Saying "thank you" is one of the most
    considerate things you can say.
Truth is the best cleanser for the soul.
Understanding is a good gift to give; it works
    for every circumstance.
Vengeance is not an option in a heart
    connected to God.
Willingness to believe is the next best thing
    to faith.
X-ray your thoughts before you say something
    you haven't thought through.
Your life is *your* life; live it well.
Zealously pray for peace, and live your life in a
    spirit of cooperation with others.

Treasure
Every
Moment

Take time each day to look at your life with thankfulness and as a gift to enjoy.

Look back on your past with an attitude of appreciation for all the lessons you've learned and a sense of gratitude as you remember every experience. Don't let regrets trouble you and steal your joy, for even less-than-welcome experiences teach us lessons and help to shape who we are.

Look to the future. Know that for every question you have and every plan you make, there is a tomorrow that will hold you gently in its arms. You will find the answers you seek.

And for the rest of your life, know that with love, acceptance, peace, and satisfaction, you will reach every goal you set for yourself and do all the things you want to do.

Always Know That You Are Loved

I wish I could give you everything you need. I wish I could make anything that's wrong be all right. I wish you could have whatever you want for whatever reason you desire. I just want you to know that I wish and hope and pray for you all the time.

When you think no one's on your side, I hope you'll remember that I am. When you need someone to believe in you, I'm on the sidelines cheering you on. I think we both know that neither time nor place would ever keep us from being there for each other, especially for something important.

I trust that you're managing your responsibilities comfortably and finding solutions to any problems you have. I hope that you have healthy relationships to give you a sense of companionship and balance. With your indomitable spirit and winning attitude, you can't lose.

My prayer is that you know you are loved, you are valued, and you are deserving. It is my fondest desire that perfect health and happiness fill your life, and I want you to know that you have my love and good wishes forever.

Choose to Live Your Life with Purpose

Remember... you've got this moment. You can choose to be happy or unhappy. You can choose what you think, what you say, and how you feel. You can choose to be hopeful or hopeless, to respond angrily or cheerfully, to be bored or interested.

You've got this day... no matter what the weather is like, you can choose what kind of day it will be—sunny or cloudy or somewhere in between. You can choose what you will do and what you won't—to give up or give in or go on. You have a choice to do something or nothing, to start now or later. You can choose your attitude about what you're facing.

You've got your life... if you're not happy, you're cheating yourself. You can talk to yourself about what you need to do to honor your life, but if you don't turn those thoughts into actions, you're just playing games.

You've got the power to make choices... your life is the manifestation of the choices you make each moment of each day. Choose to live your life with purpose.

Words to Remind You What a Great Person You Are

You're the gentlest soul, the most soft-hearted person. You help others to believe in themselves. You have compassion for those who struggle to get by.

You're the kind of person who lives your life in harmony with others—always generous, always helpful. Everyone enjoys your company!

Your endearing attitude, good nature, honesty, and caring always lift people up and show them how to be better human beings.

With you, love is more than just a word—it's a way of life. When you show love, it is on purpose.

You accept people the way they are and don't try to change them. You never act like you're better than others no matter where you are in life.

You have the kind of attitude that inspires faith and confidence and encourages people to try again when they're discouraged.

You're not afraid to show your honesty to yourself and others.

You're easy to please and easy to care about; you're comfortable in your own skin. You're dependable and fair-minded, and you give new meaning to goodwill.

You know how to be a pillar of support. You reach out, stand by, and understand. You demonstrate by example that everyone has something to contribute and there is good inside the heart of everyone.

You're such a great person, and I'm so fortunate to know you.

*Challenge
Yourself,
and Don't Ever
Settle for Less
Than Your Best*

If you have talents you're not using, discipline you haven't learned how to exercise, power you know is inside you but you haven't yet tapped into… challenge yourself. Don't settle for less when there's more of you just waiting to be revealed.

If there is a goal you want to reach, a mountain you need to move, or a door you've lost the key to… challenge yourself to reach your potential. You're capable. You have the right ideas. You just need to act on them. Go for it!

Don't wait for the spirit to move you or some miracle to drop into your lap. Find your direction; come up with a plan. Start doing what you know you should do. Start small. Start somewhere. Start now.

When something inside you tells you that you can't, don't listen. If there are doubts in your mind, they may not be real. A rose doesn't want to stay a bud forever. It wants to bloom. Fast-forward to a year from now and ask yourself where you want to be. Challenge yourself, and don't ever settle for less than your best.

Be Your
Very Best Friend

Do what is right for you. Respect your own ability to choose and to create the kind of future you want. You have all the pieces of the puzzle that you need to become the person you really want to be, but you must fit them together.

Be worthy of your own friendship. Treat yourself the way you would want someone else to treat you and the way you try to treat others. Holding resentment against yourself for mistakes you've made will only keep you stuck. In order to move on, you must have compassion for yourself and grow in maturity.

Use your creativity to build your private world. Make a deliberate effort to look on the bright side. You have many special gifts. Cultivate your talents and use your unique nature to evolve into the person you want to be. This is the only life you've got. Live it wisely and responsibly, and always be your own best friend.

May You Always Have an Angel to Guide You

May you always have an angel to help you turn every tear into a smile and to carry you on her wings when you're weak and need help. May God send you His most special angel to light up your path when the days start to look dark. When your dreams have gotten lost in the shuffle of life, may you find whatever it takes to make them come true. When doubts drown out your belief in yourself, may you have the courage to start over and the knowledge that you are capable enough to do anything you want to. You deserve so much good.

Know that you can handle anything. Don't be afraid. You're smart. Keep your confidence and determination, your humility and maturity. Stay courageous and resolute. Learn from your mistakes. Forgive yourself when you need to. Live each day as it comes. May you always have an angel to guide you.

*Dare
to Be
You!*

Trust in yourself.
Dare to be bold.
Cheer yourself on.
Celebrate every day.

Dance to your blessings.
Dream on purpose.
This is your life.
Live it your way.

Let your heart lead you.
Make yourself proud.
Mean what you say.
Love what you do.

Yesterday's gone.
Tomorrow's not here yet.
The present is now.
Dare to be you!

You're One of the Exceptional People in This World

There are some people who are so important to us that we don't know what we'd do without them. They give so much and let us give back to them. We just know they are on our side, and we wouldn't think of not trusting them. They're on our minds and in our hearts, and we're concerned about their safety and well-being. They've taught us that there is a two-way street between people who care about each other.

These exceptional people are absolutely essential for a fulfilled and balanced life. Our hearts are not satisfied without them because they share with us the big things—like happiness and love and joy.

They give their time free of charge, asking nothing in return. Their words and actions prove time and again that there's no way we could ever repay them. They've done so much and they are always going out of their way for us, without our even asking. They're easy to be with and fun to be around.

We find these people in our thoughts and prayers a lot. They're there when we need them. They share their hopefulness, appreciation, and friendliness. They give so much and care so much, and that's why they're loved so much—like you are.

You Have the Grace to Deal with Whatever Comes Along

I have seen you shoulder responsibility with just a shrug and a smile. I've watched you use your reasonable mind and tender spirit to show kindness and manage conflicts. You always do whatever you need to do. You have confidence in yourself... you change your attitude even when you can't change the circumstances.

You look closely at your troubles and never let them cause you to give up. You befriend them and learn from them so they lose their power over you. You allow them to teach you what you need to know and then move on.

You have shown before that you have inside you the strength and grace to deal with whatever comes along. Sometimes I think you don't give yourself enough credit for how much you've accomplished. In my opinion, you are a remarkable human being. Your very presence is inspiring.

There's Always Hope When You Allow Yourself to Believe

No matter how dysfunctional the world appears, look past it and follow your heart. Don't ever let the world steal your hope. Embrace life with enthusiasm every morning. Allow yourself to hope when you dream. When there's a change up ahead, open your mind to positive possibilities, no matter how you feel. Believe in miracles and choose to be happy no matter what you're going through in life.

When you try to do something and you make progress, there's hope because of your efforts. When you've been afraid but you wake up and the clouds have lifted, there's hope in the light and rest from the fears. There's always hope when you have someone to love, something to believe in, and something to do.

There's hope when you can come up with a plan and stick to it, but there's also hope if you fail a thousand times and have to start over. Start over every day if you have to. Remember... You are forgiven. You are worthy. You are loved. You can change what you need to and learn to live with what you can't change. There is hope. Believe it. Own it. Never allow yourself to be without it.

If I Could Predict the Future, Here's What I Would See for You

I see sunny days ahead, full of infinite possibilities and new adventures. I see you making graceful entrances and easy exits with lots of feel-good moments in between. I see you seizing each day, touching the sky, chasing butterflies, and making every minute count. I see you with lots of reasons to smile, wishes granted, and goals fulfilled. I see you riding on rainbows and catching stardust and moonbeams.

I see the universe cooperating and holding you in her arms, like she's protecting somebody special. I see the child in you playing hopscotch on the playground of your youth, where age is just a state of mind. I see you enjoying life and having fun.

Your Life Is a Precious Gift

Each day is like a blank canvas waiting for you
to paint the picture. If you have no idea where
to begin, just start painting. Anywhere for now
will do. You'll get your direction. You've got to
stir up the gift inside you so it will know you're
serious; then it will take you someplace you've
never been. You can't plan every move. You can't
control everything. There will be surprises. Just
trust that there's a bigger plan.

Life is beautiful, but it gets messy sometimes—
even ugly—and that's just the way it goes. You're
not going to get it all right. You'll come up with
bright ideas, but you won't follow through on all
of them. You'll learn the same old lessons over
and over and find yourself spinning in place,
getting nowhere. That's life, too, but it's just one
section on the canvas, and depending on how
you look at all the lessons you've learned, the
whole picture could really be a masterpiece.

If you give too much importance to the storms and failures and disappointments, you might be too goal oriented, and your happiness will be based on conditions. Don't ever put off being happy, even if your dreams never come true or things don't happen as you'd want them to. Dreams are important, but we are more than our dreams. Life is the prize. Things can always be worse. Be happy no matter what, and count even the tiniest blessing, for this work of art called life is the greatest gift there is.

May Your Heart Be Filled with Love and Happiness

In my treasure chest of hopes for you, I wish you the magic of laughter in your heart. I hope you feel the best you have in years and that you'll be inspired by the earth, the air, and the beauty of everything around you. Just put away your worries and enjoy every day.

I hope you'll take time to camp out in your own heart and reflect on who you are and how much you mean to others. May all the good you've done for others be returned to show you how deserving you really are.

And may you find time to sing along with the song in your heart and make your own music. Be as free as a bird. Be happy. Allow yourself to take a ride on the wings of love where you can see how awesome your life really is.

Words to Keep You Strong

When you consciously decide to let go of an old feeling that binds you and holds you back, you allow the impossible to become possible. Just by changing to a willing attitude, you shift your confidence away from fear to trust, and you allow change to happen and answers to come.

Your body, mind, and spirit want the best for you; respond to what they're telling you and try to keep them in sync.

Let your faith quiet your spirit and free your mind to make room for expanded awareness and new light. See it as a powerful source guiding you through each day and night.

You are not alone, no matter how you feel sometimes. God lives in your very own heart; He's on your side. Pray to Him often, listen to His guidance, and don't forget to thank Him for every good thing.

Sometimes there are no quick fixes. Some goals just take more time. You may have to make quite a few mistakes to make all the words and reasons rhyme.

Be who you are and let others be who they are. Don't be afraid to dream; drink from the cup of life with joy. Use every moment wisely; believe that life is good and it's on your side. Make the most of it.

My Life Is Richer
Because of You

If the definition of happiness includes having pleasant and meaningful relationships with our favorite people, then you definitely have contributed to my good fortune.

When I think about the people who are most important to me—the ones I always want to talk to, the people I trust the most, and the ones whose opinions I value—there you are at the top of the list. When I remind myself of the people with whom I can exchange my honest feelings with an unconditional freedom and without fear of being judged, I always think of you.

Not a day goes by that I don't send you good wishes, supportive thoughts, and heartfelt prayers. I really care about you, and I know you really care about me. Thank you for adding to my happiness. You are a vital part of all that I value, and my life is so much richer because of you.

No Matter Where You Are, I'll Be There for You

When you're happy about something, I hope
you'll let me share your joy with you.
In the darkness, I'll do everything I can to
lead you toward the light.
When you're finding fault with yourself, I'll
recount for you some of your strengths
and assets.
We'll be each other's lighthouse through the
storms until everything's all right.

When you're wondering which way to go, I'll
help you find the right direction.
I'll celebrate your victories with you and be
there when you're sad.

If you're confused about something, I'll be
    your sounding board and help you discover
    your own truth.
Because we're life travelers and dream sharers,
    the rough spots won't seem so bad.

When you're not who you should be, I'll remind
    you who you are.
Life is about showing others that we care about
    what they're going through.
It's about approval and encouragement for those
    who mean so much to us.
What can I say? I just hope you know by now that
    no matter where you are, I'll be there for you.

Don't Ever
Let Anything
Steal Your Joy

Choose to be well in every way. Choose to be happy no matter what. Decide that each day will be good just because you're alive. You have power over your thoughts and feelings. Don't let your circumstances dictate how you feel. Don't let your thoughts and feelings color your situation blue or desperate.

Even if you don't have everything you want, even if you're in pain or in need, you can choose to be grateful no matter what you're experiencing. You are more than your body, your physical presence, and your material possessions. You are spirit. You have your mind, heart, and soul, and there is always something to be thankful for.

Believe that the laws of the universe are impartial and you are worthy. Decide that you will live life to the fullest no matter what. Commit to changing what needs changing, but don't put off enjoying life just because you don't have everything you want right now. Steadfastly refuse to let anything steal your joy. Choose to be happy... and you will be!

Don't Forget to Play and Have a Little Fun

Having fun is not necessarily silly games—although it could be—but rather it's having a relaxed attitude about life. It means responding to the moment, factoring in a "break" time when you feel yourself getting stressed and cornered, and taking some time for yourself when you need to. It means knowing when you should work but also when you should play.

It feels good sometimes to "sneak up on yourself" and do something you hadn't planned to do at all. It could be catching up on some work you've been dreading or starting a project you haven't allowed yourself to do because you didn't think you should take the time.

When you do something just because you want to, you give your creativity the freedom to express itself and you gain a fresh perspective. That way it doesn't feel like work.

If you find yourself dreading each day, change what you're doing. Having a reason to get up in the morning enhances longevity and makes for a happier life. Your spirit needs light, your body needs rest, and your mind needs a healthy balance. Life is short. Do not underestimate the importance of having fun.

There's Power
in a
Positive Attitude

I believe there's a field of positive energy surrounding you, just waiting for you to engage it. Go play in this field. Embrace it. Give it a chance to empower you, to love you back. Interact with it. Let the light in, and let it light you up. It will help you prepare for anything you have to face in life.

Believe the best of yourself and others. Be open and willing to pamper every important wish you have, and don't let the big ones fall through the cracks. Hitch a ride on the wind, a rainbow, or a big, strong eagle in your mind—anything you can. Give yourself every chance you deserve. Think "possible," not "impossible."

Let yourself be moved to dance and sing and shout and celebrate, even if it's only in some playful space in your imagination. Go back to where you've been to understand yourself better, but don't stay in the past. Live each moment. Always smell the roses, but look ahead to where you're going and make good plans.

Swing your arms. Put a skip in your steps. Set yourself free from the don'ts. Believe. Enjoy life. It's what you were born to do.

Ten Golden Rules to Remember

1. Live your life with purpose; don't just do "whatever," or "whatever" might just be what you get.

2. Develop a compassionate spirit; you will feel better about yourself, and others will feel better about you.

3. Be honest and guard your integrity no matter what the rest of the world is doing; they're not the ones who have to live with you—you are.

4. Always do what's right; a clear conscience will keep you on the right path.

5. Be as good as your word, and don't make promises you're not going to keep.

6. Be fair to others, especially those less fortunate; there may come a time you have to walk in their shoes.

7. Adopt a can-do attitude and speak encouraging words; you'll hear them rise up in you when you need them, and others will remember them when they need lifting up.

8. Don't take your natural talents for granted. Use them to touch lives and to help you reach your highest potential.

9. When you feel discouraged or unlucky, remember the times you've been fortunate, and that knowledge will help balance out your fears.

10. Remember that what you do today will show up tomorrow, so when you make important decisions, think about tomorrow today.

There Will
Always Be a
Big Room
in My Heart
for You

You're always welcome in my heart. If you need acceptance and appreciation, you'll get it here. If you need someone to listen, I'm all ears. Here in your room, you'll have a safety net to catch you when you fall and an umbrella for when the rain is pouring down. You'll see your reflection here because your room is decorated with all the gifts you've given me... like your kindness, thoughtfulness, generosity, and understanding.

So don't ever be a stranger. The door's open... when it's springtime in your heart and you feel like celebrating and having fun, when you've got the blues in the winter or you're trying to find a refuge from the storm, when everything's perfect or when it's not... you're invited to come in and stay awhile.

And guess what? You always have a standing reservation.

I Have So Many Hopes for You

My first hope is that you're taking time out for you. Life is so busy for everyone now, and I know it's hard to find time for everything. You do so much for others that you would probably be the first one you'd neglect. So… I hope you're finding time for yourself.

I think of you every day and send you warm thoughts. I lift you up in prayer and ask that your needs be met and that every dark cloud turns into a guiding star. I hope the people who are important to you are there for you. I hope there are smiles and laughter to fill your days, contentment in each moment, and joy beyond description.

If there are lessons you need to learn, I hope you can learn them. If there are places you want to go, I hope you'll go. If there are mountains you need to move, I hope you will. Most of all, I wish you a heart filled with optimism and expectation to inspire and attract everything good that life offers.

This is my prayer and my dream for you for the rest of your life.

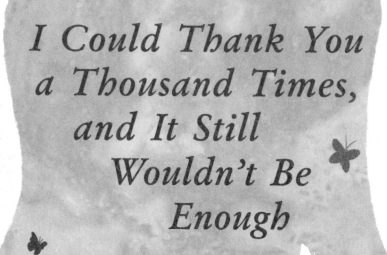

I Could Thank You
a Thousand Times,
and It Still
Wouldn't Be
Enough

Thank you for sharing your time. Thank you for your generosity, unselfishness, and goodwill.

Thank you for being so easy to communicate with. Your willingness to lend a helping hand is so appreciated. You probably think nothing of it because it is your nature to want to help others. But even that attitude is a credit to you, too.

Your actions remind me to care more and to be more considerate of others. You have taught me so many valuable lessons about life. I will always be inspired by your example, and your thoughtfulness is not something I take for granted.

Thank you for being such a good teacher. For all the wonderful things you do, I hope each kindness you have given is someday returned to you.

I Prayed
for You Today

I prayed for you today, gave thanks for your life, wished you the best, asked the heavens to bless you with good health and happiness. I sent you good thoughts, surrounded you with hope and faith and love. I asked your guardian angels to protect you and keep you safe from any harm and to blanket you with joy and contentment and peace and prosperity.

I prayed for you today. I asked that you be guided to make choices that enhance your life and changes that are in your best interest. I wished for you a storehouse of opportunities, the ability to meet your goals, and the joy of your own approval and acceptance. I wished for you your heart's desire, every need met, every prayer answered, and every dream come true.

I prayed for you today. I asked that you be prepared for whatever life hands you or whatever you're going through. I asked that your spirit be strong and lead you and guide you each step of the way down every path you take. I asked the universe to confirm for you that you're someone very special. I asked the earth to be good to you, and I asked God to show you His perfect way. I prayed for you today.

*Always
and Forever...*

May you reach every goal you've set for yourself. May perfect opportunities come your way. May your days be filled with good fortune, good health, abundance, and joy. May you have the wisdom and understanding to do whatever makes you happiest, and may every dream you long for come true.

I want you to know that I'm here for you... to listen and to help... to share the laughter and the heartache, the boredom and the blues... to celebrate the craziness and the delight when something big is going on. I'm also here when life is not all that pretty. We're close enough to be honest with each other all the time, and I'm thankful that we're in each other's life.

In all the ways that matter most, appreciate the gift of your life because you are truly somebody special. May your tomorrows hold new beginnings for you, and may your future be bright. May the satisfaction of every lesson learned and every goal reached advance your feeling of fulfillment and keep you on a positive path.

May All These Wonderful Blessings Be Yours...

The Gift of Love

May you love and be loved by the people who mean the most to you. Allow love to give you a constant sense of balance and soulful and spiritual nourishment.

Good Health

May you be physically, mentally, and emotionally well, and may you have the wisdom and ability to maintain good health all the days of your life.

A Joyful Heart

May your attitude about life lead you to love others, as well as yourself. May it help you deal with whatever you encounter in life: success, failure, pleasure, disappointment, and all the in-betweens.

The Loyalty of Family

May you have a supportive family... people to go home to... people close to you who know where you came from and where you are now... people who care about you just as you care about them.

The Treasure of Friendship

May you have friends who enrich your life, want the best for you, and support you the way you always do for them.

Genuine Happiness

May you always have the freedom and opportunity to express yourself creatively so you can be who you want to be. When you need reassurance, may you turn your fears into faith and your doubts into trust. Happiness is your birthright. Claim it.

I'm So Blessed
to Have Someone
in My Life
as Special as You

We have shared so much... good times and bad times and hopes and fears and dreams. We reach out and reach back, and we've come to depend on each other. I believe we will always be close.

You have such a unique spirit; your kindness is given free of charge, with no strings attached. You are gracious, forgiving, and a pleasure to be around. You make a positive difference in the life of every person you touch.

You shine your light wherever you go. I know you want the best for me. You make me feel supported and cared for, and your confidence in me helps me to have a little more faith in myself. I can't remember a time that you weren't there for me.

Exceptional people like you are as dependable as the stars that shine at night, and I am so blessed to have someone in my life as special as you. Always remember that you are loved, you are cared about, and I thank God for you... every day.

About the Author

With her first album, *The Happiest Girl in the Whole U.S.A.*, which achieved platinum album status and earned her a Grammy, Donna Fargo established herself as an award-winning singer, songwriter, and performer. Her credits include seven Academy of Country Music awards, five Billboard awards, fifteen Broadcast Music Incorporated (BMI) writing awards, and two National Association of Recording Merchandisers awards for best-selling artist. She has also been honored by the Country Music Association, the National Academy of Recording Arts and Sciences, and the Music Operators of America, and she was the first inductee into the North America Country Music Association's International Hall of Fame. As a writer, her most coveted awards, in addition to the Robert J. Burton Award that she won for "Most Performed Song of the Year," are her Million-Airs Awards, presented to writers of songs that achieve the blockbuster status of one million or more performances.

Prior to achieving superstardom and becoming one of the most prolific songwriters in Nashville, Donna was a high school English teacher. It is her love of the English language and her desire to communicate sincere and honest emotions that compelled Donna to try her hand at writing something other than song lyrics. Donna's other books include *I Prayed for You Today* and *10 Golden Rules for Living in This Crazy, Mixed-Up World*. Her writings also appear on Blue Mountain Arts greeting cards, calendars, and other gift items.